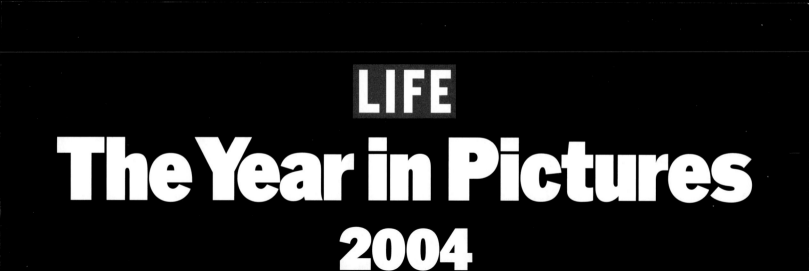

LIFE
The Year in Pictures
2004

Displaced Sudanese take refuge from the heat of day and potential enemies.

LIFE
The Year in Pictures

LIFE Books

Editor Robert Andreas
Director of Photography Barbara Baker Burrows
Creative Director Lynda D'Amico
Deputy Picture Editor Christina Lieberman
Writer-Reporters Hildegard Anderson (Chief), Adriana Gardella
Copy Wendy Williams (Chief), Christine Q. Brennan, Lesley Gaspar
Production Manager Michael Roseman
Assistant Production Managers Leenda Bonilla, Rachel Hendrik
Photo Assistant Joshua Colow
Consulting Picture Editors
Mimi Murphy (Rome), Tala Skari (Paris)

Editorial Director Robert Sullivan

President Andrew Blau
Finance Director Craig Ettinger
Assistant Finance Manager Karen Tortora

Editorial Operations Richard K. Prue (Director),
Richard Shaffer (Manager), Brian Fellows, Raphael Joa,
Stanley E. Moyse (Supervisors), Nora Jupiter (Assistant
Manager, International), Keith Aurelio, Gregg Baker,
Silvia Casta eda Contreras, Trang Ba Chuong, Charlotte Coco,
Erin Collity, Scott Dvorin, Osmar Escalona, Kevin Hart,
Rosalie Khan, Sandra Maupin, Po Fung Ng, Barry Pribula,
Carina A. Rosario, Albert Ruffino, Christopher Scala
David Spatz, Vaune Trachtman, David Weiner

Time Inc. Home Entertainment

President Rob Gursha
Vice President, New Product Development Richard Fraiman
Executive Director, Marketing Services Carol Pittard
Director, Retail & Special Sales Tom Mifsud
Director of Finance Tricia Griffin
Marketing Director Ann Marie Doherty
Prepress Manager Emily Rabin
Book Production Manager Jonathan Polsky

Special thanks to Bozena Bannett, Alexandra Bliss,
Bernadette Corbie, Robert Dente, Anne-Michelle Gallero,
Peter Harper, Suzanne Janso, Robert Marasco, Natalie McCrea,
Brooke McGuire, Margarita Quiogue, Mary Jane Rigoroso,
Steven Sandonato

Published by

LIFE Books

Time Inc.
1271 Avenue of the Americas,
New York, NY 10020

ISBN: 1-932273-52-2
ISSN: 1092-0463
Library of Congress Control
Number: 2004108514

"LIFE" is a trademark of
Time Inc.

We welcome your comments
and suggestions about LIFE
Books. Please write to us at:
LIFE Books, Attention:
Book Editors, PO Box 11016,
Des Moines, IA 50336-1016

If you would like to order any
of our hardcover Collector's
Edition books, please call us
at 1-800-327-6388 (Monday
through Friday, 7:00 a.m.–
8:00 p.m., or Saturday, 7:00
a.m.–6:00 p.m., Central Time).

Please visit us, and sample
past editions of LIFE, at
www.LIFE.com.

Classic images from the pages and covers of LIFE are now
available. Posters can be ordered at www.LIFEposters.com. Fine
art prints from the LIFE Picture Collection and the LIFE Gallery
of Photography can be viewed at www.LIFEphotographs.com.

On November 20, a British armored
personnel carrier from the Black Watch
battle group returns to its base, Camp
Dogwood, 25 miles south of Baghdad.

A Time of Discord

It was a year of cold comforts. Abroad, the war in Iraq festered day after day, and news from other fronts offered little solace. At home, the election seemed to divide rather than unite . . . Oh, to be a Bostonian.

Seeing the above image of an Iraqi prisoner in Abu Ghraib who had been told he would be electrocuted if he stepped off the box was perhaps the low point of the year for many Americans. In a moment seemingly from another world, Olympic gymnastic champion Carly Patterson is embraced by her coach, Evgeny Marchenko.

In some respects, 2004 was like a flashback to 1967. Once again, the country was locked in a distant war that seemed to be getting worse instead of better. Politics were sharply divided along party lines, and the two sides seemed more eager to shout than to discuss their differences. Tens of thousands of protesters took to the streets. And, with an infrequency rivaling that of Halley's Comet, the Boston Red Sox were appearing in the World Series.

Regardless of whether you thought the war in Iraq was a good idea, the news from there was consistently demoralizing. It was said that the road to democracy was being paved there, but nevertheless it seemed each morning brought another grim tale of casualties. When the talk wasn't about a mounting death toll, it concerned issues such as soldiers refusing to go on patrol, questions about the lack of bulletproof vests, tales of recalled soldiers who thought they had already fulfilled their commitment. Then, when the story of Abu Ghraib prison broke and we saw the sordid pictures of Americans humiliating their prisoners, it was a blow that was, quite simply, difficult to absorb.

There were, to be sure, signal examples of valor, of sacrifice, of devotion, of honor. And how difficult it was when each night the *CBS Evening News* ran a little bio of fallen heroes, for every one of these kids seemed so very special, and such a loss for the nation.

Speaking of the network news shows, changes of the guard were afoot. Tom Brokaw said his good-byes late in the year, and Dan Rather, perhaps somewhat less voluntarily, announced that he would

Smiley Pool/Dallas Morning News

leave his post in 2005. These sorts of changes are important: Most Americans get their news from these half-hour shows. And the anchors are the media when it comes to important events, like war, like the hurricanes that beset us for so long, like a presidential election.

The battle between incumbent President George W. Bush and Democratic nominee Senator John Kerry was fascinating, bitter, incendiary and way too close to call until the very end. When it was all over, it still seemed like half the country was happy, the other half not. It remains to be seen whether the President can, with his second term, win over some of the disaffected.

Rancor was evident even in the field of entertainment, as Mel Gibson's *The Passion of the Christ* was awe-inspiring for many but condemned by others. The Olympics made for a wonderful festival, yet even this celebration of international amity was clouded by fears of terrorism. A professional basketball game in suburban Detroit turned into an ugly melee that caused some to wonder if sports in this country are headed for the sort of spectator fiascoes one encounters on other continents.

That would be a dismal prospect indeed. With

Pitcher Keith Foulke and catcher Jason Varitek exult after the Red Sox sweep the World Series. At left, golfers in Palm Beach Gardens, Fla., play through an early moment in Hurricane Frances.

few exceptions, the field of sports has provided Americans, a notably hardworking people, with a well-earned respite, in which fans at home and in the stands can kick back and enjoy themselves for a few hours.

At least that's how it has been in most places. For sports fans in and around The Hub of the Universe, however, a certain pleasure has been a long, long time coming. Since 1918, actually. But that harrowing dry spell has at last come to an end, and in old Beantown the cry could finally ring out: the Boston Red Sox, World Champions of 2004!

Winter

Mongolian Sleigh Ride

This competition is part of a winter festival held in northern China's Inner Mongolia region that attracts tourists from Beijing, Hong Kong and elsewhere from late December through January. The camel race—by the way, the two humps make them Bactrian camels—is a traditional activity of the Ewenki people. The festival also features many other attractions, such as an ice ballet, skiing, ice fishing and even a beauty contest.

Photograph by EPA/Landov

An Ill Wind

Africa's largest country, the Sudan is characterized by rock desert, undulating sand dunes, vast swamps and extreme heat. It is also characterized by malaria, tuberculosis, illiteracy and, since its independence in 1956, alternating periods of ineffective parliamentary rule and military governance. To make dire matters yet worse, civil conflict has become epidemic as the Muslim majority in the north tries to dominate the animist and Christian peoples of the south. As a result, the economy, such as it is, is withering, and famine in the south is ubiquitous, as are officially sanctioned amputations and stonings. The chaos has displaced millions, like this woman, adrift in a temporary "settlement" in the Darfur region, bent by the ravages of time and place.

Photograph by Olivier Jobard Sipa

❝ There are strong indications that war crimes and crimes against humanity have occurred in Darfur on a large and systematic scale. ❞

—**Kofi Annan,** U.N. Secretary General

Jan. 1 A pediatric journal reports that **American teenagers are fatter** than those of 14 other industrialized nations. The study of 30,000 teens found that some 15 percent of U.S. youngsters are obese and roughly 30 percent are "modestly overweight."

Jan. 3 "This is a big night for NASA. We are back!" says administrator Sean O'Keefe after the Mars exploration rover, Spirit, lands on **the Red Planet.** The eight-month mission will look for geological evidence that water once flowed on our neighboring planet. The timing is right: Earth and Mars will be closer than at any other time in recorded history.

Hawaiian Cruise

Surfers never dream small, but it was left to one man to surpass all that had come before. On January 10, Pete Cabrinha, a 42-year-old veteran of crests and pipelines, caught and rode out a wave off Maui that was the highest ever surfed and recorded: 70 feet. Mastering the massive swell garnered Cabrinha the 2004 Billabong XXL prize of $70,000. Next up for the daredevils of the surf is the Holy Grail—a 100-foot wave.

Photograph by Eric Aeder Billabong XXL

❝ It was growing in front of me and growing behind me, so it felt like I wasn't getting anywhere. ❞

—**Pete Cabrinha**

Jan. 5 After 14 years, former baseball great Pete Rose admits that **he bet on baseball** while he was managing the Cincinnati Reds. "I'm sorry for all the people, fans and family that it hurt," Rose says, shortly before his book *Pete Rose: My Prison Without Bars* goes on sale.

Jan. 8 The AMBER Plan, initiated in 1996 to broadcast warnings in **child abduction cases,** helps Georgia police officers catch Jerry William Jones, 31, accused of kidnapping three girls and killing three adults and a 10-month-old. A motorist spotted the car and phoned the police, who caught Jones after he crashed into a utility pole. The girls were safely reunited with their mother.

Jan. 12 Three young men plead guilty in Richmond to vandalizing SUVs, fast-food eateries and construction sites. The trio made the attacks while in high school on behalf of the **Earth Liberation Front,** which is devoted to protecting the environment and preventing urban sprawl.

The Face of Art

Switzerland is famous for its lighter-than-air pastry, but here it seems that a Dutch visitor shows the Swiss that they are not alone in serving up heavenly delights. For the 26th International Hot Air Balloon Week, held at Château-d'Oex, a ski resort in the Swiss Alps, more than 130 balloons from 20 countries take to the air. Moments before his turn, Vincent is clearly itching to Gogh.

Photograph by Laurent Gillieron AP

Jan. 16 The U.S. Central Command announces that an investigation "has been initiated into reported incidents of detainee abuse" at Abu Ghraib prison, outside of Baghdad. **Shameful** accounts and lurid photographs of the tortured inmates and their abusers appear on front pages of newspapers across the world. On May 7, U.S. Secretary of Defense Donald Rumsfeld goes to Congress to offer his "deepest apology" but refuses to resign.

Jan. 20 The Salvation Army is the recipient of the **largest known donation** ever made to a charity, $1.5 billion. McDonald's heiress Joan Kroc, who died in 2003, left the bequest in her estate. "After we get up off the floor," says W. Todd Bassett, the commander in chief of the SA, "we have a tremendous amount of work to do."

Jan. 21 *Trail*, Britain's most popular hiking magazine, expresses regrets for giving readers **bad instructions.** Climbers following the publication's directions for descent from Ben Nevis, Great Britain's tallest peak, would have been led off the edge of the north face of the mountain.

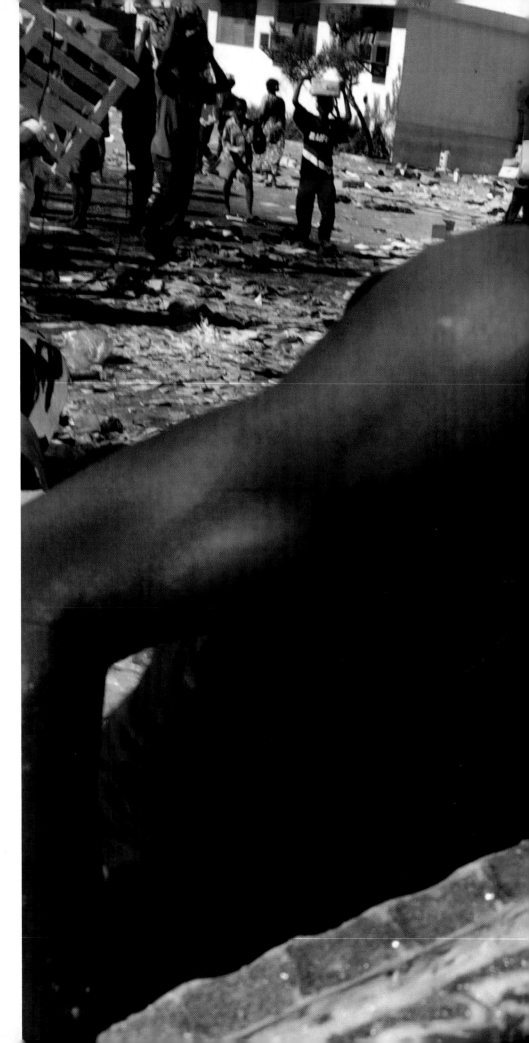

Mean Streets

The small Caribbean nation of Haiti has had more than its share of woes. For many years the people have had to endure relentless poverty ensured by brutal leaders such as Papa Doc and Baby Doc Duvalier, dictators whose notion of largesse was to occasionally drive through the streets, tossing out crumpled wads of small-denomination bills. It seemed as though help might finally have arrived in the person of Jean-Bertrand Aristide, a former priest who, in 1990, became the country's first democratically elected president. But this was not to be. Ultimately, he was every bit as corrupt and malevolent as his predecessors. Finally, on February 29, in the wake of fierce fighting between rebels and his thugs, and bowing to external diplomatic pressures, Aristide fled to Africa. Days later the streets of the capital city, Port-au-Prince, were in chaos, as desperate Haitians sought to survive until the next debacle.

Photograph by Shaul Schwarz Corbis

Jan. 25 Break-dancers from his native Poland put on a performance for Pope John Paul II, 83, at the Vatican. Watching from a raised throne, **the pontiff waves his hand** after each dancer completes a routine of leaping, flipping and spinning his body to the beat of a boom box.

Feb. 1 Claiming their second NFL championship in three years, the **New England Patriots** defeat the Carolina Panthers 32–29 in Super Bowl XXXVIII.

Feb. 8 Singer Beyoncé Knowles walks away with five **Grammy Awards,** including one for Best R&B Album, *Dangerously in Love.* The 22-year-old ties the record for the most Grammys won by a female artist.

Tying the Knot

In a year marked by intense divisiveness in America, the topic of same-sex marriage was yet another lightning rod for dissension. Marriages of men to men and women to women suddenly began receiving enormous attention as they sprouted up in such communities as Portland, Ore., New Paltz, N.Y., and San Francisco. From February 12 to March 11, more than 4,000 Bay Area couples acquired wedding licenses. (Here, outside City Hall, Siddiqui Ray is lifted by her new spouse, Liz McElhinney.) Then on March 11, the California Supreme Court temporarily halted the issuing of such licenses. Following much legal wrangling and opinion offering, voters finally spoke up on Election Day, when all 11 states that included a ballot to outlaw gay and lesbian marriages passed the ban by substantial margins.

Photograph by Kimberly White Reuters

Feb. 10 While Luke Tresoglavic, 22, is snorkeling amid coral reefs on the coast of New South Wales, Australia, a two-foot wobbegong shark bites him in the leg and **won't let go.** Tresoglavic swims 300 yards to shore and drives to a local surf club— with the wobbegong still attached. A clever lifeguard finally makes the shark let go by flushing its gills with fresh water. With 70 needlelike punctures in his leg, Tresoglavic then drives to a nearby hospital, taking the dead shark with him.

Feb. 12 Yet another celebrity romance comes undone; this time it's Ken and Barbie, **"the perfect plastic couple,"** who are splitting after 43 years. They met on a TV commercial for the Mattel toy company in 1961 and had been together ever since.

Toil and Trouble

Long before the current state of affairs existed in Iraq, it was a land that relied heavily on oil. Now that the colossal endeavor to rebuild the nation is underway, fossil fuel is expected to finance the recovery and provide perhaps 95 percent of the new government's revenues. But sabotage to pipelines and refineries across the country have steadily increased since late February, when this major line near Karbala, 60 miles south of Baghdad, was set ablaze. Iraqi policemen stand guard, but the damage has already been done.

Photograph by Faleh Kheiber Reuters

❝ Add the poor shape to begin with and what is happening now on the ground, and you have a very, very crippled industry. ❞

—**Dr. Gal Luft,** Institute for the Analysis of Global Security

Feb. 17 Five thousand miles from its home in the Amazon, a piranha is fished out of the Thames River. A seagull is thought to have dropped the **fierce, razor-toothed fish** onto the deck of a boat east of London, whose owner then tossed it into the water. Since piranhas can't survive in cold water, it died, but still bore the marks from the seagull's beak.

Feb. 23 Two 700-year-old **mummies,** a boy and a man in his thirties, go on display at the National Institute of Culture in Peru. Even though they predate the Incas, they are so well preserved that one has an eye and internal organs intact. Later in the year, thousands of Inca mummies, some bundled together in groups, are unearthed in an ancient cemetery near Lima.

Tears and Rain

In the deadliest terrorist attack to hit Europe since 1988's airliner sabotage over Lockerbie, Scotland, a series of 10 explosions were detonated on four Madrid commuter trains during the morning rush hour on March 11, killing 191 people. Evidence pointed to extremist Islamic groups, particularly because Osama bin Laden had earlier threatened to seek revenge on any nation, like Spain, that joined with the U.S. in the Iraq war. Here, millions gather in the capital city to protest against the slaughter. A couple of days later, however, voters opted for an antiwar candidate who promised to withdraw Spanish troops from Iraq.

Photograph by Pierre-Philippe Marcou
AFP/Getty

Feb. 24 A 6.5-magnitude quake strikes northern Morocco, claiming nearly 600 lives and injuring 300 more, many of them **asleep in their mud-brick homes.** The quake is so strong that it roils the Strait of Gibraltar, off Morocco's northern coast.

Feb. 24 A sixth-grader in Belpre, Ohio, is suspended from school for three days for bringing *Sports Illustrated*'s **swimsuit issue** to gym class. He is cited for violating the school's policy on nonverbal harassment and possession of lewd or suggestive material.

Feb. 29 In a perfect sweep, *The Lord of the Rings: The Return of the King* wins all 11 **Oscars** for which it is nominated, including Best Picture.

March 5 Martha Stewart is convicted of **obstructing justice and lying** about her ImClone stock sale. She is sentenced to five months in prison, five months of home confinement and is fined $30,000. The 62-year-old turns herself in to the Alderson Federal Prison Camp in West Virginia on October 8, vowing to return to work in time to start planting her spring garden.

Precautions in the Plains

Such is the state of affairs today that we might not be surprised to see a collection of people testing these strange outfits in Los Angeles, say, or Miami or New York. But that this picture was taken in Casper, Wyo., does give one pause. These fire-fighters are trying out new Haz Mat (hazardous material) suits designed to protect against flash fires and chemical poisons. Although Wyoming appears to be a low-risk state for terrorist activity, some residents there worry that any place in America could fall prey to a cataclysmic event.

Photograph by Steve Liss Time

❝ Attacking a rural target may actually instill more fear by delivering the message that no one is safe. ❞

—**Peter Beering,** terrorism expert, in *First to Arrive*

March 10 Before long, the Big Dipper and other constellations may have new neighbors. Alexander Lavrynov, a Russian spacecraft designer, has patented a device that will put product ads into space. By linking satellites equipped with sunlight reflectors, he plans to create messages **visible from Earth.**

March 13 Hoping to make the *Guinness Book of World Records*, a housepainter from Alexandria, Ind., unveils his masterpiece, **a 1,300-pound baseball**—a green one. For 27 years, Michael Carmichael went home from work, walked to a shed behind his house and commenced painting. After 18,000 layers, the ball has grown to be more than 35 inches in diameter. Declares Carmichael: "I am not going to start any more baseballs."

A Troubling Incident

Another step deeper into the dark hole that is Iraq came at the end of March when four American civilians were killed and burned. Two were then hanged from this bridge spanning the Euphrates River in Fallujah, a nest of virulent anti-U.S. sentiment that lies to the west of Baghdad. Later in the year, Fallujah would be attacked by Coalition forces. The victims were employees of Blackwater Security Consulting, one of many firms that are assisting the American military in Iraq.

Photograph by Khalid Mohammed AP

March 17 After a nationwide manhunt, alleged **Ohio sniper** Charles A. McCoy Jr., 28, is arrested in a Las Vegas motel. He is the lead suspect in two dozen shootings that killed a woman and terrorized motorists on highways around Columbus.

March 27 An experimental X-43A pilotless plane breaks the world speed record for an atmospheric engine, reaching 5,000 mph, or more than **seven times the speed of sound.** The craft was dropped from the wing of a B-52. The successful launch by NASA comes 57 years after Chuck Yeager broke the sound barrier. In November, an X-43A very nearly reaches 10 times the speed of sound.

March 31 Low-fare carrier JetBlue launches an **Airplane Yoga** program "designed to bring fitness and inner peace to the skies." Inside each seatback pocket is a card that offers instructions for four yoga poses that passengers can execute without leaving their seats.

"Queen Mary 2"

What would it take to restore steamship-era glamour and excitement to the sometimes tacky diversion of cruise ship travel? Nothing short of the *Queen Mary 2,* an $800-million eyepopper that enchanted admirers on both sides of the Atlantic when she first set sail.

PA Photos

Dave Caulkin/AP

Hail, "Mary"

Although the world's largest passenger ship was touched by tragedy when more than a dozen people died after a gangway collapsed during construction, the mood here is celebratory as the 1,132-foot liner departs on January 12 from Southampton, England, amid cheering onlookers and fireworks. Above: At a ceremony attended by Cunard President Pamela Conover and Comdr. Ronald Warwick, Queen Elizabeth II christens the vessel named for her grandmother Queen Mary. Taking over the transatlantic route previously traveled by sister ship *Queen Elizabeth 2, QM2* has a staff and crew of more than 1,200, ready and able to pamper 2,600 passengers.

Carlos Guevara/Reuters

Queen Giant

More is, well, more on board *QM2* (above, anchored in the Canary Islands), with its five swimming pools, 10 restaurants and the world's first on-ship planetarium, which doubles as a movie theater. Opposite, the great ship seems outsized even in the context of a New York City streetscape.

G. Fabiano/Sipa

PORTRAIT **Mel Gibson**

As a risk-it-all action hero, he has been one of Hollywood's biggest stars for the past 20 years. He has also been an Oscar-winning director. This time out, he followed his heart, and took the chance of his career.

Chosen by Gibson for his "otherworldly" quality, devout Catholic Jim Caviezel suffered his own ordeals while playing Jesus. During filming, the actor dislocated his shoulder and was struck by lightning.

Newmarket/Everett Collection

Nina Berman/Redux

The critics were divided and so were moviegoers. Mel Gibson's *The Passion of the Christ* opened on Ash Wednesday, and across the land the response was little short of visceral, as one Statesboro, Ga., couple can attest: After seeing the film, an argument between the husband and wife over a theological point left them both injured—and charged with battery.

The dramatization of Jesus' final hours seemed like box office poison to Hollywood, so studios passed on distribution rights. While *Passion* boasted Gibson (as director, cowriter and coproducer), there were no car chases, sex scenes or meet-cute story lines. What's more, viewers were forced into the netherworld of subtitles, as Gibson had the actors speak in Latin and Aramaic. This was hardly the terrain of *Lethal Weapon.* But the onetime holder of *People* magazine's Sexiest Man Alive title was determined to screen his vision—even if it took a decade and $30 million of his own funds.

Born in Peekskill, N.Y., on January 3, 1956, Mel was the sixth of 11 children; the family moved to Australia in 1968. Once a night hound, Gibson now attends Mass daily in his own chapel. He claims *Passion* grew from a near-suicidal period that he survived by meditating on Jesus' torment: "I had to use the Passion of Christ to heal my wounds."

In the days before the film's release, Gibson's father, Hutton, made anti-Semitic remarks during a radio interview, maintaining that the Holocaust was largely fictional. When Mel refused to denounce—or support—his father's views, the furor escalated. Although some Jews felt that the film was fair, others complained that Jews were stereotyped and depicted as Christ-killers. Many non-Jews were appalled by the relentless brutality of the story, but for a lot of believers, the blow-by-blow interpretation was revelatory.

In the end, *Passion* grossed more than $20 million on its opening day, and revenues would surpass $600 million worldwide, a rare success for an independent film. But then, this was a movie that was rare in and of itself, a historical saga replete with tunics and spears, but one that actually was about an article of faith—certainly for some.

"I think we have gotten too used to seeing pretty crosses on the wall, and we forget what really happened," said Gibson in defense of the intense images that earned *Passion* an R rating.

Spring

A Cause for Celebration

This picture was taken in the Johannesburg Botanic Garden, located in the wealthy northern suburb of Emmarentia. It used to be reserved exclusively for white people. Then, 10 years ago, South Africa held its first democratic election, and now people of any race can have their wedding ceremonies at this lovely site. Here, in this image, is a splendid manifestation of the sort of beauty that freedom can engender.

Photograph by Jodi Bieber/NB Pictures/Contact

Easter Message

After attending Easter Sunday services with his family in Fort Hood, Tex., President Bush pauses to talk with the inevitable gathering of reporters. He is responding to questions about a recently released briefing memo from August 6, 2001, that warned al-Qaeda was active in the U.S. and could resort to hijacking planes. At the rear stands then National Security Adviser Condoleezza Rice, and it seems rather apparent that she has one thought she is trying to communicate to her boss: "Mr. President, come over here right this minute and get in the car . . ."

Photograph by Luke Frazza AFP/Getty

April 2 "The court has no choice but to declare a mistrial at this time," states the judge presiding over the six-month-long **fraud trial** of two former Tyco International executives. Deliberations reach an impasse after a juror receives a threatening letter.

April 5 Thousands of villagers, many traveling hundreds of miles, **pay their respects to a dead whale** washed up on a beach in southern Vietnam.

April 6 UConn becomes the first school to win the **men's and women's national NCAA basketball titles** in the same year. Diana Taurasi helps her teammates topple Tennessee 70–61 the day after the men knock out Georgia Tech 82–73.

April 15 Wearing a wet suit and lugging an air tank, diving gear and a backpack full of cash, a robber is nabbed by police before he can make his **liquid getaway.** The 35-year-old man held up an Olympia, Wash., bank with an assault rifle, then stripped down to his aquatic wear and headed for Budd Inlet, where the officers netted him.

SHREK
icebreaker.com

A Sheep in Wool Clothing

On April 16 a woman who was walking the Bendigo sheep station in New Zealand saw something that stopped her in her tracks. It turned out to be a merino sheep that had escaped from its domestic flock six years earlier and, since that time, had successfully avoided annual shearings by hiding out in caves. Newly nicknamed Shrek, the 10-year-old ram (here, with sheep musterer Daniel Devine) caused a sensation in the sheep-happy country, and when he was finally sheared, the process aired live on television. The result was 60 pounds of fine merino wool, which was earmarked for an auction to benefit children's medical charities.

Photograph by Stephen Jaquiery
Otago Daily Times/AP

Inset: Simon Baker Reuters

❝ He looked like some biblical creature. ❞

—**John Perriam,** Bendigo station owner

April 23 A volume of **phony Hitler "diaries"** is auctioned off for $7,741 in Berlin. First published by the German magazine *Stern* in 1983 for $4.8 million, they were soon declared fake by experts and the forger was sent to prison.

April 26 The **500-year-old Leonardo da Vinci masterpiece** known as the *Mona Lisa* is beginning to show its age. The thin poplar panel on which it was painted has become deformed and is causing Louvre officials "some worry." A week later it is announced that the portrait will be X-rayed, but the museum promises that "analyses will take place in such a way as to allow the work to remain on public display" for the six million visitors who view it each year.

The Tides of Time

May 12, Palestine: Another day in the region is defined by the familiar theme of attack and retaliation. In this instance, following a confrontation, the Israeli army has cut off the road from Gaza City to Khan Yunis. So it is that these people must resort to making their way along the beach, and their means of travel seems as timeless as the conflict itself.

Photograph from Abbas/Magnum

April 29 The National World War II Memorial, honoring the 16 million who served in the U.S. armed forces in that conflict, opens on Washington's Mall. The **granite-and-bronze monument** features waterfalls, fountains and a wall adorned with gold stars representing the more than 400,000 Americans who died in the war.

April 29 In a Somerset, N.J., courtroom, former nurse Charles Cullen, 44, **pleads guilty to killing 14 patients** in hospitals in New Jersey and Pennsylvania. When arrested, he claimed responsibility for a string of 30 to 40 deaths.

May 11 A gruesome video on an Islamic Web site shows the beheading of Nicholas Berg, a 26-year-old Pennsylvania contractor missing in Iraq since April. **The execution** by five masked militants is said to be revenge for U.S. abuses committed at Abu Ghraib prison. Decapitation of foreigners becomes a frightening tactic in the war.

May 12 **Billions, perhaps trillions,** of cicadas are awakening from their 17-year slumber and will soon start to swarm across 14 eastern states in what may well be the largest insect emergence in history.

The Grief That Is War

The 3rd Battalion, 112th Field Artillery has a proud history. Known as the New Jersey Guns, the unit, headquartered in Morristown, N.J., dates back to the Revolutionary War, when, under an earlier name, it fought with George Washington at Trenton. During World War II, it saw action in the breakthrough of St. Lo. In 2004, the unit served in Iraq as part of the First Cavalry. In two separate attacks in Baghdad, on June 4 and 5, four soldiers from this National Guard outfit were killed. This soldier was uninjured but mourns the loss of his fallen comrades.

Photograph by Robert King Zuma

May 14 Syracuse University will install sensors in the Seneca River and five lakes that are water sources for more than 500,000 people in central New York. These **underwater robots,** beaming up a profile of lakes, rivers and reservoirs, may one day help protect the nation's drinking water from sabotage.

May 18 A small **moon rock** worth about $5 million is stolen from Malta's Museum of Natural History. Found in a lunar valley by *Apollo 17* in 1972, the sample was given to Malta by President Richard Nixon.

May 21 Pemba Dorji, a Nepalese Sherpa, breaks the record for **the ascent of Mount Everest** by more than two hours. He scales the 29,035 feet in eight hours and 10 minutes, a feat that took Sir Edmund Hillary and Tenzing Norgay seven weeks to accomplish in 1953.

May 24 At the Army War College in Carlisle, Pa., President Bush warns that **"difficult days are ahead"** in Iraq. He proposes a five-step blueprint to return control to the Iraqis and says that 138,000 troops will stay "as long as necessary." The handover of sovereignty is completed on June 28, two days ahead of schedule.

The One That Got Away

Not since Secretariat in 1973 had a horse so captivated Americans. Smarty Jones was born at Someday Farm, outside of Philadelphia, and as a two-year-old survived a fractured skull and severe damage to his left eye. However, after being handed over to trainer John Servis, the colt won his first six races handily, and in the seventh, took the roses at the Kentucky Derby. The Preakness posed no problem, as he romped home by 11 lengths. Then, with everyone pulling for Smarty to be the first horse since 1978 to win the Triple Crown, the mile and a half of the Belmont Stakes proved too much, and he faded, losing to long-shot Birdstone. Smarty would retire because of sore hooves, but for a while, he was just the tonic a gloomy nation needed.

Photograph by Heinz Kluetmeier
Sports Illustrated

❝ He ran hard and did a great job. We didn't get the total outcome that we wanted, but we had a really good ride. ❞

— John Servis

June 3 Bowing to severe criticism over **questionable intelligence** on Iraq, George Tenet, 51, resigns as director of the CIA.

June 9 Thirteen oil firms are organizing an exercise on how to clean up oil spills with **popcorn,** which, after it absorbs water, forms an emulsion similar to oil. When the popcorn is dumped off Norway's coast, 30 boats and observation aircraft will respond in the practice drill.

That Longest Day

June 6 marked the 60th anniversary of one of the world's most famous, and remarkable, events: D-Day. It is astonishing that the largest invasion in history—involving 10,000 planes, thousands of ships and landing craft, and 156,000 troops—one that would create the Second Front in Europe in World War II, could have remained a secret despite ceaseless efforts by the enemy to ferret out the destination. That locale was, of course, Normandy, on the coast of France. The ultimate success of D-Day secured victory for the Allies in Europe, although it was a hellish experience. The anniversary in 2004 was marked by the appearance of presidents and prime ministers, of course, but also by the return of some of the men who actually engaged in the terrible combat. Here, an American veteran pauses, perhaps recalling an old buddy.

Photograph from Gamma

June 11 A teacher in Rochester, N.Y., is put on paid leave after **washing out a third-grader's mouth with soap.** When the boy made a "vile, very nasty sexual reference" to a classmate, he was taken to the nurse's office and a drop of soap was placed on his lower lip and washed off immediately with the warning never to repeat such language. "Old-fashioned ways work," said the unapologetic teacher.

June 14 The U.S. Supreme Court votes 8–0 to let **"under God"** stay in the Pledge of Allegiance. But the justices sidestep the question of whether the pledge is unconstitutional because it may violate the separation of church and state.

Come Fly with Me!

The first time he departed a plane in midair, as a Navy pilot shot down during World War II, he forgot to get free from the aircraft before pulling the rip cord on his parachute. He ended up with a nasty blow to the head when he hit the plane, though he lived to tell about it. This time there were no mistakes, but then, age does bring wisdom, and after all, former President George H.W. Bush was making this jump to celebrate his 80th birthday. Here, with an audience below that included wife Barbara and former Soviet President Mikhail Gorbachev, he is accompanied by the United States Army's Golden Knights parachute squad.

Photograph from U.S. Army AP

 **I like speed.**

—**George H.W. Bush**

June 17 The 9-11 Commission finds that U.S. officials were **unprepared "in every respect"** to prevent the hijackings that killed nearly 3,000 people. Five weeks later it issues a report chronicling the failures of the CIA, FBI and other intelligence agencies.

June 22 "It's like adult *Harry Potter* mania," says one bookseller after Bill Clinton's ***My Life*** flies off the shelves at stores. The 957-page memoir, priced at $35, sells more than 400,000 copies the first day, believed to be a record for nonfiction.

June 25 Michael Moore's *Fahrenheit 9/11* appears on more than 800 screens across the country amid controversy. Winner of the Cannes Film Festival's Palme d'Or, the **"docu-tragicomedy"** is a blistering assault on the Bush administration before and after the historic 2001 attack.

FOCUS ON | A Rave New World

Images delivered from the vantage point of space provide glimpses into the heretofore unseen, and make some of our distant neighbors both more familiar and more startling.

Our Universe Expands
Cameras on board the Hubble Space Telescope send back images of what is known as the Hubble Ultra Deep Field. Containing an estimated 10,000 galaxies, it is the deepest portrait we have ever had of the visible universe.

NASA (3)

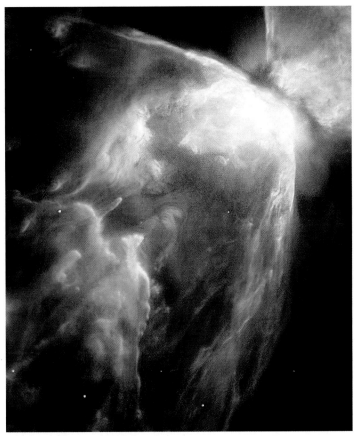

Big Doings

A dying star (above, captured by the Hubble Space Telescope) makes a dramatic exit 4,000 light-years from Earth. Its red-hot remains are shrouded by the Bug Nebula, which is a mass of gas and dust. Below, the remnants of the exploded star Cassiopeia A are vividly observed by Chandra, an X-ray observatory that was launched into space in 1999 aboard the *Columbia* space shuttle.

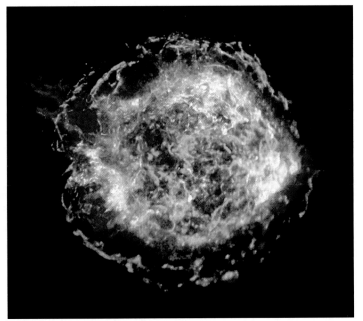

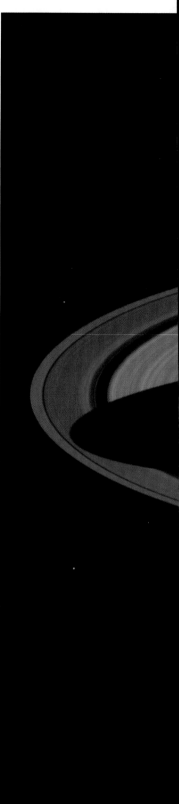

Going Ringside

The Cassini spacecraft, part of a cooperative mission involving NASA and two European space agencies, is the first ever to orbit Saturn. It was launched in 1997 and, finally, in 2004, began its scheduled four-year tour of the planet. Cassini's cameras take us closer than ever before to the second-largest planet, although the photo above, of Saturn's equatorial band, was nevertheless taken from a distance of 14.5 million miles. At right, Saturn's groovy rings, which, according to one scientist, are largely composed of ice and mud-like gunk, are delineated.

NASA (3)

A Sight for the Ages

Like a splendiferous spherical specter, Saturn, which is nearly 900 million miles from Earth, floats, here, 17.6 million miles from Cassini's lenses. Almost 10 times the diameter of our planet, Saturn and its rings are seen in a panoramic view created by combining two narrow-angle camera pictures. Truly one of the greatest photographic images ever recorded.

Taking a Stroll on Mars

In addition to IMAX-quality pictures (above, rocky terrain on the Red Planet) and weather reports, the latest robotic visitors to Mars have sent back evidence that water once flowed there. Twin rovers Spirit and Opportunity traversed the Martian landscape—and performed better than their less mobile counterparts had on previous missions. At right, Clovis rock, bearing an impression left by Spirit, yielded signs of interaction with water. Future missions will hunt for evidence of life.

Cosmic Bling

It's a vision befitting a jewelry catalogue, but this glittering bracelet is composed of blue star clusters, not diamonds. Encircling the gold-toned nucleus of a former galaxy, it is bigger than the Milky Way and lies 300 million light-years away. This shot makes the image appear close at hand. It comes courtesy of the Hubble Space Telescope, which on April 24 celebrated the 14th anniversary of its launch.

Pete Souza

PORTRAIT

Nancy Reagan

Though her golden years with Ronnie were not what anyone would have hoped for, she made sure her final moments with him were all they could be. Along the way, the erstwhile actress and former First Lady earned her most glowing reviews, for her courage and grace.

Whisper-thin, she was a mite slowed by the infirmities that can come with age. But during a long week of pageantry honoring her late husband, Nancy Reagan was the embodiment of fortitude. The woman who, despite sweeping popularity, once drew fire for her sway over him (informed at times by her astrologer, no less) and her displays of recession-era opulence, earned the admiration of Americans across the political spectrum. "We love you, Mrs. Reagan," many cheered as they watched her bid adieu to the man she had stood by for better and worse—indeed, what proved to be much worse.

Married since 1952, the former First Lady and her Ronnie built a relationship that deserved applause, even a standing ovation. Their style may have been too mushy for some, but it was honest. "On my birthday, he always sent my mother flowers to thank her for having me," she wrote. Ronald, devastated by his divorce from actress Jane Wyman, often gushed that he did not become whole again until he married Nancy. His equally effusive bride said, "My life really began when I married my husband."

Born Anne Frances Robbins on July 6, 1921, Nancy suffered when her parents divorced soon after her birth. She was adopted at the age of 10 by her stepfather, Chicago neurosurgeon Loyal Davis. Following graduation from Smith College, she became an actress and appeared in 11 films, including *Hellcats of the Navy* opposite Reagan. But after they wed, Nancy quit Hollywood and voiced no regrets.

She played the role of First Lady with élan. Outfitted in Adolfo, preferably red, she adorned the presidency in high style. There was substance, too. Though her "Just Say No" antidrug campaign was often derided as simplistic, she was, without question, committed to the cause.

A traditional wife and mother, she nonetheless had her husband's ear on policy matters. Each relied on the other. "Reagan doesn't worry about anything, so Nancy worries

about everything," joked their friend Barry Diller.

Over the years, there was much happiness, but also plenty to worry about: The President was badly wounded in a 1981 assassination attempt. Later, he was diagnosed with colon cancer, then prostate cancer and skin cancer. Nancy survived breast cancer, undergoing a mastectomy in 1987. Then came the ultimate trial: In 1994, Reagan learned he had Alzheimer's. With hopes of raising awareness, the former First Couple shared the news with the world. As always, Nancy focused on protecting her husband, allowing few to witness his decline. Friends recall that, for a decade, she rarely left the house for lunch. It was impossibly cruel that in his final years Ronnie no longer seemed to recognize her.

Though she spoke at the 1996 Republican National Convention, Nancy won't tow the GOP line on embryonic stem-cell research—a possible key to an Alzheimer's cure. Her efforts to persuade the Bush administration to support this science have so far failed, but her dissenting voice is there.

Dealing with the week-long ceremony and cross-country travel might have overwhelmed someone half her age, and yet she was remarkable. The funeral was a tribute she had long planned, reviewing the details annually, down to her husband's backward-facing boots on a riderless horse.

She now begins life without Ronnie, and we can only hope there are brighter days ahead for her. That is exactly what he would have envisioned.

Mrs. Reagan received dignitaries at Blair House, the official guest residence across the street from the White House. Clockwise from left: former Soviet President Mikhail Gorbachev; President George W. Bush; Britain's Prince Charles; and former British Prime Minister Margaret Thatcher. Nancy, Ron Jr. and his wife, Doria, gaze at the cornfields of Tampico, Ill., Reagan's birthplace, as a 747 carries them home to California following the Washington, D.C., service.

Saying her goodbyes: as viewed from the dome of the U.S.
Capitol (left), and at the Ronald Reagan Library and
Museum, in Simi Valley, Calif., where Navy Capt. James
Symonds presents Mrs. Reagan with the flag that had,
moments before, draped her husband's casket.

TRIUMPH

VERY LIFE

Bryan Chan/Los Angeles Times

Summer

Prime Seasonal Fare

Dinner has just ended at Echo Hill Camp in Maryland, on the eastern shore of Chesapeake Bay, and for dessert these 14-year-old tentmates have opted for a sweet delivery from on high.

Photograph by Ronna Gradus

The Halls of Justice

In his first public appearance since he was captured and deposed in December 2003, Saddam Hussein is arraigned on July 1 in a courtroom in Camp Victory, Iraq, and the proceedings are broadcast on Iraqi television. Saddam appears by turns nervous and defiant. He is charged with war crimes and genocide.

Photograph by Karen Ballard Redux

❝ You know that this is all a theater by Bush, the criminal, to help him with his campaign. ❞

—**Saddam Hussein**

July 3 In a stunning upset at Wimbledon, Russia's Maria Sharapova dethrones two-time defending champion Serena Williams, 6–1, 6–4. **"I knew that the power was within me,"** says the 17-year-old.

July 6 The Democratic presidential campaign revs up after John Kerry selects fellow senator **John Edwards,** 51, from North Carolina, as his running mate: "I have chosen a man who understands and defends the values of America."

July 7 Scientists reveal that they have unearthed the largest collection of **dinosaur fossils** ever found in Germany. The fragments may date back 130 million years, and some could belong to a previously unknown species.

July 8 Kenneth Lay, 62, former **Enron** chairman and CEO, pleads not guilty to 11 charges related to his firm's collapse in 2001. He surrenders to the FBI in Houston a day after being indicted by a grand jury and is released on $500,000 bail.

Running Wild

Tradition has it that this city in northeast Spain was founded in 75 B.C. by the great Roman general Pompey as a military settlement. Originally it was named after him, but through the years the name has shifted to its present form: Pamplona. Each July, the Fiesta de San Fermín is held, and daily bullfights are preceded by the "enclosing" of the bulls, as they are run through the streets amidst daredevil men and boys. Here, on the first morning, a bull slides as it rounds a corner.

Photograph by Dani Cardona Reuters

> **" Pamplona is no place to bring your wife. "**
>
> —**Ernest Hemingway,**
> *A Dangerous Summer*

July 16 More than 80 children die in a fire at a private school in Kumbakonam, India. The blaze begins in the kitchen, then reaches the **illegal thatched roof** of the building, trapping students in a room with just one exit. More than 200 schools are soon closed for inspection.

July 19 A 182-carat **diamond**—four times the size of the famous Hope diamond—is deposited for safekeeping in the vaults of Guinea's Central Bank. A 25-year-old miner dug up the stone in a forest of this West African nation.

July 19 Finding their cell doors accidentally left unlocked, four inmates from the Hawkins County Jail in Rogersville, Tenn., head for a local market and buy **four cases of beer.** When they return with their suds they are charged with escaping and introducing intoxicants to the prison.

Uh . . . Don't Look Down

After years of designs and debates and construction, a viaduct crossing the Tarn River valley near the town of Millau in southern France was at last completed in 2004. The structure provides the finishing touch to a motorway running from Paris to Barcelona. At 1,125 feet it is the world's tallest bridge—taller even than the Eiffel Tower. At about a mile and a half long, it is an architectural and engineering marvel, the first cable-stayed bridge built with seven pylons rather than two or three.

Photograph by Stephane Compoint

July 21 A videotape shows four of five **September 11 hijackers** passing security checks at Dulles International Airport shortly before boarding American Airlines Flight 77, the plane they would crash into the Pentagon.

July 21 Cambridge University physicist Stephen Hawking, 62, reverses the assertion he made 30 years ago that once matter "disappears" within **a black hole,** it leaves no trace. He now concludes that objects can escape from a black hole.

July 22 After interviewing more than 1,000 witnesses and poring over two million documents, the 9-11 Commission publishes its 567-page report. Warning that **"we are not safe,"** the panel calls for a sweeping overhaul of intelligence and a cabinet-level national director.

July 25 Wearing the yellow jersey, Lance Armstrong, 32, clinches his record sixth straight Tour de France win after crossing the finish line in Paris. **"You're awesome,"** says fellow Texan George W. Bush.

July 29 Protected by a $60-million security blanket, John Kerry accepts his party's presidential nomination at the **Democratic National Convention** in Boston.

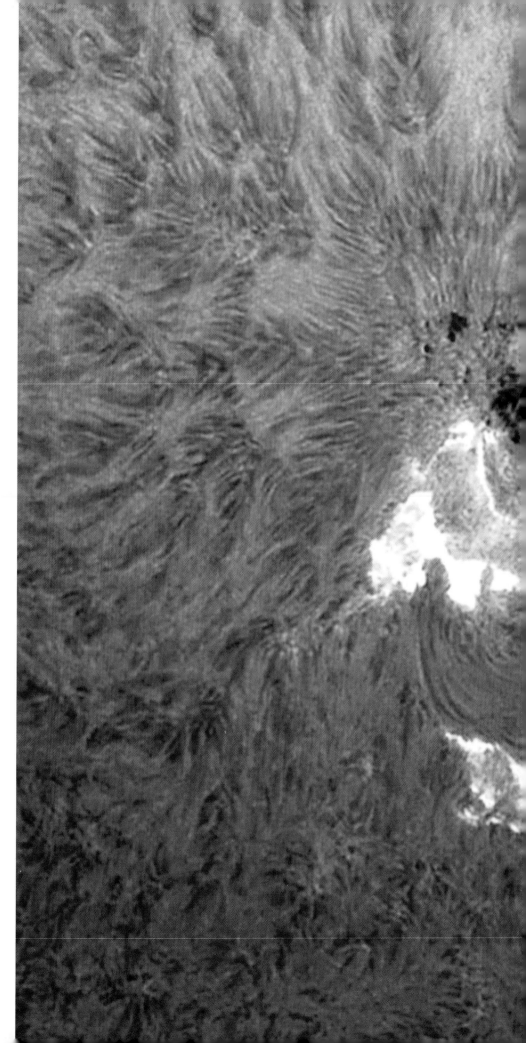

Solar Blast

This otherworldly image, which was taken on July 22, shows activity above massive sunspot 652. Actually a mix of spots construed as one, sunspot 652 at this point was about 20 times the size of Earth. A sunspot is a vortex of gas on the surface of the sun that involves tremendous magnetic activity. It is capable of wreaking havoc on satellites and power grids. Why it occurs is open to conjecture.

Photograph by Jack Newton

July 30 "Now you can 'stick' Arnie," Austrian television tells viewers after a one-euro postage stamp featuring California Governor **Arnold Schwarzenegger** goes on sale in honor of his 57th birthday. Demand for the stamp is heavy.

Aug. 1 A fire turns a crowded shopping center in Asunción, Paraguay, into an inferno, leaving more than 400 dead. It begins when **grease in a charcoal grill** ignites at a supermarket.

Aug. 1 Fears of terrorist **attacks against financial institutions** in New York City, Washington, D.C., and New Jersey raise the threat level from yellow to orange. Laptop computers belonging to an al-Qaeda leader indicate that the financial services sector may be a target for new assaults. Although it is later learned that the information may have been dated, the precaution lasts until November 10, when the level is lowered back to yellow.

Aug. 3 The **Statue of Liberty** opens for the first time since September 11, 2001. Measures have been taken to tighten security for this international symbol of freedom and hope.

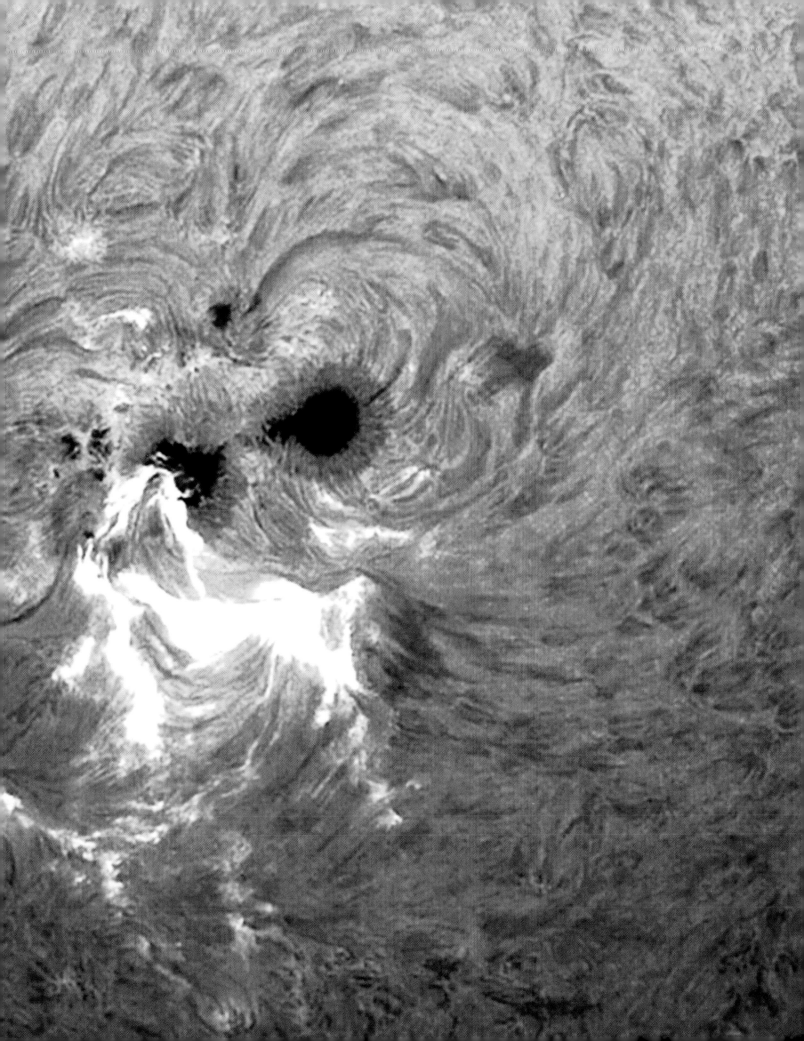

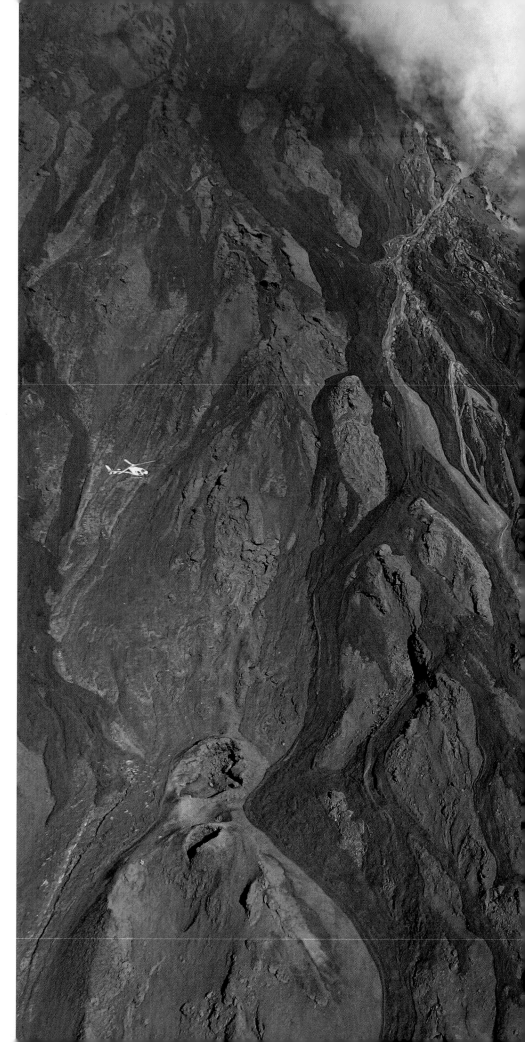

Rivers of Fire

The island of Réunion lies in the Indian Ocean, a few hundred miles east of Madagascar. It is a rather forbidding place, of volcanic origin, studded with mountains. Since 1925, one mountain's crater, known as Piton de la Fournaise, has been active any number of times. In fact, it is now one of the world's most active volcanoes, erupting about every six months. The fissures seen here, on August 13, are riddled with lava, but they are at the top of the volcano and, so far, the island's population has remained unharmed.

Photograph by Richard Bouhet AFP/Getty

Aug. 4 While George Bush and John Kerry are campaigning for votes at separate rallies in Davenport, Iowa, robbers strike **three of the town's banks.** "I'm sure they were counting on the fact that we were shorthanded," says one member of the local police force, "but we weren't." Arrests are made in two of the thefts.

Aug. 8 At the Gorilla Foundation in Woodside, Calif., 12 specialists come to the aid of Koko, a 33-year-old gorilla with a bad toothache. Schooled in **sign language** since she was a baby, Koko points to the problem and the caretakers extract the troublesome tooth.

Aug. 12 Faced with a potential sexual harassment lawsuit by a former male aide, New Jersey Governor James McGreevey, 47, **admits that he is gay** and has had an adulterous affair with a man. Married and the father of two, McGreevey resigns on November 15.

Aug. 24 Almost simultaneously, **two Russian airliners,** some 450 miles apart, explode. Suicide bombers are blamed for the disasters, which claim 89 lives.

Shallow Grave

Humpback whales breed north of Rio de Janeiro, so the sight of them from nearby beaches is not uncommon. But when the big mammals actually reach the shore, that is another matter. Here, on August 9, sea biologists and fire department workers are trying to save a humpback whale on the Rio Branco beach, not far from the city. As humpbacks go, this young male was on the small side, at 33 feet and 10 tons, but still a huge creature. For three days a hundred rescuers tried everything, even tugboats, to pull the tired animal out to sea, but in the end their valiant efforts failed, as the whale's weight had placed too much pressure on his organs.

Photograph by Vanderlei Almeida
AFP/Getty

Aug. 30 The **GOP National Convention** opens in New York City to renominate President Bush and Vice President Cheney. Protesters march through Manhattan to express their opposition to the war in Iraq.

Sept. 1 The **rape case** against basketball star Kobe Bryant is dismissed in Eagle, Colo., after his accuser declines to testify. Bryant says, "Although I truly believe this encounter between us was consensual, I recognize now that she did not."

Sept. 2 A devastating fire at the Duchess Anna Amalia Library in Weimar, Germany, destroys 50,000 **irreplaceable volumes** from the 16th, 17th and 18th centuries. However, workers form a human chain and save 6,000 works, including a 1534 Bible that belonged to Martin Luther.

Sept. 6 After suffering chest pains and shortness of breath, former President Bill Clinton, 58, undergoes a quadruple coronary artery operation in New York City. Seven weeks later he is **up and about, stumping** for John Kerry in Philadelphia.

Tiny Victims

It was a brutal week for Russia. First, nine people were killed outside a subway station by a suicide bomber. Then two airliners were blown up, killing everyone aboard. But what came last was the worst: In a grotesque three-day standoff that began on September 1, Muslim terrorists held a school in Beslan hostage, and in the end, perhaps 350 people were killed, about half of them children. The images of the scorched and battered survivors were indelible. Tons of aid flooded in from many nations, but the grief and mourning from this will go on for a long, long time.

Photograph by Konstantin Zavrazhin
Gamma

> **We showed weakness, and weak people are beaten.**
>
> —**Vladimir Putin,** Russian president

Sept. 7 The death toll for U.S. military personnel in Iraq surpasses 1,000, **a grim milestone** in the 18-month war. More than half of those killed had not yet celebrated their 30th birthday.

Sept. 15 Five protesters push their way into the British House of Commons in an effort to prevent lawmakers from banning the centuries-old practice of **fox hunting with dogs.** After a brief recess, the debate resumes and ends with a vote of 356–166 in favor of outlawing the practice.

Sept. 16 The United States Mint unveils **two new nickels** to commemorate the Lewis and Clark expedition. A different profile of their sponsor, Thomas Jefferson, appears on the front, while the reverse will feature either a redesigned buffalo or a view of the Pacific Ocean. The coins will enter circulation in 2005.

Wind, Water, Woe

There surely have been rough hurricane season before, but the blows of 2004 seemed as bad as any in recent memory. Charley, Frances, Ivan—all major storms that took a terrible toll in lives and monies lost—were accompanied by several other weather systems that created their own problems or just scared people half to death. The folks in Florida and several Caribbean nations seemed to be constantly on the ropes, and there were plenty of other places that were hit hard as well. A season we'd like to forget, but unfortunately will long remember.

Photograph by Douglas R. Clifford
St. Petersburg Times

Sept. 19 On Emmy night, *The Sopranos*, widely considered one of the best shows on TV, wins its first Best Drama award, but *Angels in America* is **the star of the evening,** with 11 trophies. Meryl Streep and Al Pacino take Best Actress and Actor honors for their roles in the miniseries.

Sept. 20 "We made **a mistake in judgment,** and for that I am sorry," Dan Rather informs viewers of *60 Minutes*, admitting that the network was unable to authenticate documents that alleged President Bush had received preferential treatment while in the National Guard. Rather later announces that he will leave his post as the news anchor for CBS.

Sept. 27 The Taj Mahal, **India's shrine of love,** begins a six-month celebration of its 350th birthday with a flight of pigeons and a kite contest, followed by a classical music concert at sunset.

Sept. 27 Researchers at a Louisville, Ky., hospital and other sites are treating stroke victims with an anticlotting drug derived from **vampire bats.** A protein in the bat's saliva prevents the blood it drinks from clotting, and doctors hope it may have the same effect on humans.

FOCUS ON The Olympics

More than a century had passed since the Games were last held in Athens. This time, some things were quite different, but one constant remained: the spectacle of young athletes giving entirely of themselves.

The Wheels of Time
Cycling was an event in the inaugural Modern Olympics in Athens in 1896, although only men competed back then. Here, in 2004, women zip past the Acropolis during the 118.8-kilometer event, which was won by Sara Carrigan of Australia. Security measures for these Olympics were unprecedented, and although the fortnight passed without violence, attendance was light due to fears of terrorism.

George Tiedemann

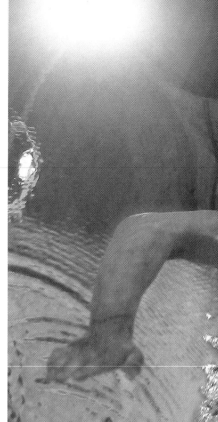

Scott Barbour/Getty

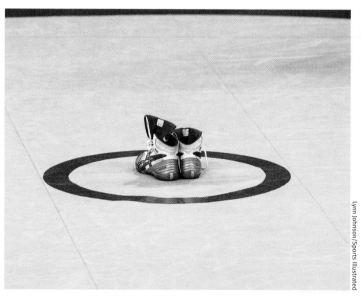

Lynn Johnson/Sports Illustrated

Total Commitment

At top, Irina Korzhanenko summons every last bit of strength as she puts the shot during the women's finals. The Russian's effort earned her the gold medal. Above: Rulon Gardner of Wyoming did a cartwheel when he won the gold as a superheavyweight wrestler in Sydney in 2000. This time around he failed in his bid to repeat, but was still proud of winning a bronze. Afterward, in the traditional gesture of farewell to his sport, he left his shoes behind: "To leave them on the mat meant I left everything on the mat as a wrestler."

Amid the Swirl

At left, Australian Grant Hackett competes in the finals of the 4x200-meter freestyle relay, in which the Aussies placed second to the United States. Hackett, however, did win the gold in the 1,500-meter individual freestyle. American swimmer Michael Phelps failed to break Mark Spitz's record of seven gold medals, though he did win six. Bottom center: The U.S. women's softball team celebrates a 5–1 victory over Australia in the championship game, as the head coach from Down Under, Simon Roskvist, makes the long walk across the infield. Below: Brazilian Vanderlei de Lima was the favorite to win the marathon, and he might have done so if defrocked Irish priest Cornelius Horan had not chosen this moment to make another one (Wimbledon, Grand Prix races) of his bizarre public disruptions. Horan received a suspended sentence from the courts, while de Lima settled for a bronze.

Afterglow

Any athletes who have the extraordinary skills and determination to make it to the Olympics will be happy to confide that they want nothing more than to be at the Games and to do the best that they can. And this statement will be true. However, every single one of them also wants to win—that's what it means to be a world-class competitor. The young men and women on these pages made it to the top of the mountain. Opposite, top: American Carly Patterson is beaming as she displays her pride and joy, which she earned for being the best all-around female gymnast at Athens. Bottom: What better time to capture a moment than on the winners' podium? From left, the Games' top competitors in the women's 100-meter breaststroke—Leisel Jones of Australia (bronze), Luo Xuejuan of China (gold) and Brooke Hanson of Australia (silver). At left, belaureled Paul Hamm of the U.S. wears the gold medal awarded to the all-around champion in men's gymnastics. It was later determined that South Korea's Yang Tae Young should have received a higher point total than Hamm, but the International Olympic Committee elected not to reverse the decision.

Smiley Pool/Dallas Morning News

Michael Mulvey/Dallas Morning News

Team "SpaceShipOne"

It sounded like a reality-TV-show gimmick: The first privately funded team to design and successfully fly a plane into space twice within two weeks will get $10 million. But for a group of true believers in the California desert, it was real life.

When I first saw it, I thought he'd lost his mind," said test pilot Mike Melvill. He was talking about boss Burt Rutan's design for *Space-ShipOne,* the trailblazing craft that has opened the way for space tourism. But the founder of Scaled Composites, a Mojave, Calif.–based aerospace company, truly had his wits about him.

It started in 1996 when the X Prize was announced. (It was later renamed the Ansari X Prize

to acknowledge a multimillion-dollar donation from entrepreneurs Anousheh and Amir Ansari.) The goal was to jump-start commercial space travel, much as earlier aviation awards helped launch today's airline industry. Rutan, who once called NASA "the other space agency," was eager to dive in. After he teamed with investor and Microsoft cofounder Paul Allen in 2001, the race was on.

On September 29, 2004, Melvill piloted *Space-ShipOne* on its first qualifying flight from Earth's atmosphere. Traveling at 2,200 mph, the round-trip

Rutan checks for mail at his Mojave, Calif., home. The "box" was fashioned from the wing of an earlier creation. Mike Melvill (above) and Brian Binnie (below) in *SpaceShipOne*'s cockpit make final preparations before taking off and reaching a peak altitude of 70 miles above our planet.

to blackest space took less than two hours. Melvill's colleague Brian Binnie clinched the prize on October 4, 2004, when he helmed the craft on its second flight, beating out more than 20 teams.

SpaceShipOne, named the Coolest Invention of 2004 by *Time,* opens up space travel to ordinary, if deep-pocketed, citizens. By 2007, Virgin's Richard Branson hopes to offer wannabe astronauts a trip to space on a modified version of the plane, for a mere $190,000. More than 7,000 space-seekers (including William Shatner) are on the waiting list.

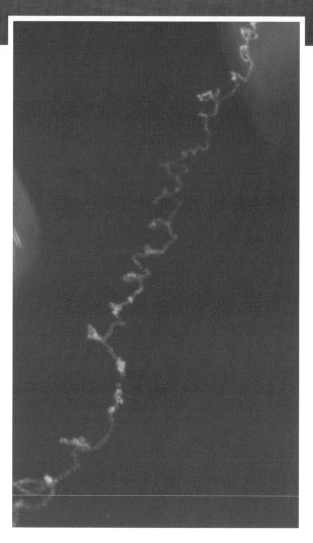

Investor Amir Ansari checks out Melvill's progress from a chase plane. Top: *SpaceShipOne* is hooked to the belly of the mother ship, *White Knight*. After an hour-long climb, the launch aircraft releases the smaller plane, which then travels independently. Nearing the top of its flight, with Melvill at the controls, the craft makes a series of unscripted spirals (right), terrifying those watching from the ground, who include aviator Charles Lindbergh's grandson. Melvill, however, is unruffled: "That was a really good ride. I feel like I nailed it." Opposite: Telescopic tracking allows astronomers to follow *SpaceShipOne*'s flight even after it leaves Earth's atmosphere.

Melvill's wife, Sally, inspects her wedding ring after it returns from its trip into space with her husband. Mike and Sally were, respectively, Scaled Composites' second and third employees. Below, Melvill is greeted by the legendary Scott Crossfield, who, as an aeronautical research pilot back in 1953, was the first man to fly at twice the speed of sound. Opposite: Melvill and Binnie congratulate each other on a job well done. Binnie rides atop *SpaceShipOne* following his suborbital flight. The term *suborbital* refers to a mission that leaves the atmosphere yet doesn't muster enough speed to continuously orbit Earth.

Mark Greenberg/WorldPictureNews (3)

Fall

A Vision for the Ages

The Northern Lights, or aurora borealis,
are caused by an interaction between
solar particles and the atmosphere near
the North Pole. However, the exact
mechanisms behind the display are still
something of a mystery. What is certain,
though, is that anyone who has witnessed
the Lights—as here, in Skarsvag,
Norway—will not soon forget them.

Photograph from LAIF

A Long Wait

For this happy young girl, the idea of standing in line to vote undoubtedly seems ordinary. But for these others, on October 9, this is quite an event: Afghanistan's first democratic presidential election. The transitional president, Hamid Karzai, emerged the winner, though he faces tremendous problems in the ravaged land. Terrorism, corruption and the drug trade have all taken deep root here, and numerous other societal situations are unchanged, as is evident from this queue of women who are still pressured to wear the head-to-toe burka.

Photograph by Yunghi Kim Contact

❝ This was a commendable election, particularly given the challenging circumstances. ❞

—**An investigating panel of foreign experts**

Oct. 1 A plume of steam and ash rises 10,000 feet above Mount St. Helens, but it dissipates in less than an hour. The next day, the volcano-alert level is raised to **"eruption imminent,"** then subsequently lowered. Scientists maintain a close watch on the mountain, which is either building a dome or rebuilding its cone.

Oct. 4 London's Heathrow Airport installs a new X-ray machine that uses low-level radiation to **see through passengers' clothing.** Dubbed a "voyeur's charter" by civil liberties advocates, the device will enable security officials to spot hidden weapons and explosives. Comments one passenger: "It's all about being safe, and I really have no problem with it."

Enchanting but Ominous

The Harding ice field in Alaska's Kenai Fjords National Park is ablaze in color, which is lovely, except that this picture was taken in the fall. On November 8, the findings of the Arctic Climate Impact Assessment (ACIA), an important four-year study, were released. A research team found that temperatures in the Arctic have risen nearly twice as fast as elsewhere, and over the next hundred years they will likely melt at least half the Arctic sea ice. This could threaten the security of indigenous cultures, flood low-lying areas in Florida and Louisiana, affect currents and regional climates, and play havoc with such creatures as polar bears, caribou and walruses. The main causes are fossil fuels and greenhouse gases, says the study.

Photograph by Ashley Cooper
Picimpact/Corbis

❝ The impacts of climate change on the region and the globe are projected to increase substantially in the years to come. ❞

—**Robert Corell,** chairman, ACIA

Oct. 5 "We profoundly . . . regret that we will be unable to meet public health needs this season," says Howard Pien, CEO of Chiron Corporation, after British regulators halt the manufacture of **influenza vaccine** at the company's Liverpool plant. The shortfall will reduce the U.S. supply by half and could cost businesses $20 billion in worker absenteeism.

Oct. 8 Hoping to do away with **polio** forever, the World Health Organization launches a huge immunization drive in 23 countries in sub-Saharan Africa. More than a million workers will vaccinate 80 million children, the single largest public health program in history.

Joy in Beantown

It had been a long time, since 1918. In between had come four seasons—1946, '67, '75, '86—in which, each year, they had lost a heartbreaking seventh game. It seemed there would be no chance this year, not when they were down three games to none to the detested New York Yankees in the playoffs. No team had ever come back from that margin. But the 2004 Red Sox could, and did. And after that the Cardinals were a four-game breeze in the World Series. Here was one time when not only Bostonians, but the downtrodden everywhere could take cheer: The Curse was no more.

Photograph by Mike Blake Reuters

❝ We did it! ❞
—**Manny Ramirez,** World Series MVP

Oct. 11 With the corn as high as an elephant's eye, more and more farmers are converting some of their fields into **maize mazes.** Intricate patterns replicate, for example, a lobster (in Maine) or portraits of Bush and Kerry (in Utah). Some difficult courses have guides in overhead towers to help stymied clients find their way out.

Oct. 12 Fearing that terror attacks **could harm visitors** and his staff, Senator Mark Dayton of Minnesota closes his Capitol Hill office until after the election. Although there seemed to be no indication of an imminent threat, Dayton said he had "no second thoughts" about his action.

Oct. 20 ABC drops the **Miss America** show, leaving the annual beauty and talent pageant without a TV network for the first time in 50 years. The decision comes after this year's installment drew only 9.8 million viewers, a record low. "It's certainly an ominous sign," observes Leonard Horn, a former pageant CEO.

Our New Family Member

Two Australian researchers stunned the world of science when they announced in the pages of *Nature* that they had uncovered a new humanlike species that grew only to the size of a three-year-old modern human and had a very small brain. The find, which could revise the history of human evolution, was made in a cave on Flores Island, 350 miles east of Bali: a nearly complete skeleton of a three-foot-tall 30-year-old woman (dubbed the Hobbit) who lived some 18,000 years ago, and parts of six other skeletons, one from as recently as 13,000 years ago. *Homo floriensis* joins Neanderthals as the only hominids to coexist with *Homo sapiens*. It is possible that "hobbits" and humans interacted on Flores Island.

Photograph from AP
Inset: Stephen Hird Reuters

Oct. 24 The interim Iraqi government and the U.N. Nuclear Agency say that nearly 380 tons of powerful nonnuclear **explosives have vanished** from a storage site that was supposed to be under U.S. control. The whereabouts of the missing material, strong enough to bring down buildings, make missile warheads and detonate nuclear weapons, are unknown.

Oct. 26 To celebrate her 150th birthday, the USS *Constellation,* the only **Civil War–era vessel** still seaworthy, embarks from Baltimore's Inner Harbor for a 30-mile sail to Annapolis. Aided by tugboats, the ship, festooned with red, white and blue flags, reaches the Naval Academy, where a brass band, roaring cannons and cheering onlookers greet her arrival.

Nov. 2 After one of the **most bitterly fought presidential campaigns** in recent history, George W. Bush is reelected, with 286 electoral votes to John Kerry's 252 — and roughly three million more popular votes than his opponent.

Trial of the Year

This was one of those murder cases that grab the country by the throat. On Christmas Eve, 2002, Scott Peterson, a fertilizer salesman from Modesto, Calif., told police that his pregnant wife, Laci, was missing. Thus was set in motion nearly two years of police work, accusations, a trial engulfed by voyeuristic news coverage, and a developing portrait of a world-class lowlife. In the end there was no smoking gun, but the preponderance of evidence, perhaps buttressed by the lack of apparent emotion in the defendant, led on November 12 to a conviction of first-degree murder for the death of Laci and second-degree for the unborn Conner.

Photograph by David Paul Morris Getty

Nov. 2 Democrats have something to cheer about: the charismatic U.S. Senator-elect from Illinois, **Barack Obama.** Rising to prominence after his stirring keynote address at the Democratic National Convention, the 43-year-old Obama will be the only black to serve in the Senate in 2005 and just the fifth in Senate history.

Nov. 9 A **Cabinet reshuffle** begins with the resignation of Attorney General John Ashcroft and Commerce Secretary Don Evans. Six days later, they are followed by Secretary of State Colin Powell and three others. On Nov. 16, President Bush nominates his National Security Adviser, Condoleezza Rice, to succeed Powell.

Nov. 14 "We have definitely found it," says American researcher Robert Sarmast, claiming that he and a team of explorers have located **Atlantis** in a Mediterranean seabed between Cyprus and Syria. Deep-water sonar scanning indicates man-made walls fitting the description of the acropolis at Atlantis, an island civilization that the Greek philosopher Plato believed existed some 11,500 years ago.

Mourning in Ramallah

Throngs of supporters of the late Palestinian leader Yasir Arafat await the arrival of his body at his compound in Ramallah, where he had spent the past few years, essentially as a prisoner of the Israelis. He had succumbed in Paris on November 11 to an unknown disease and would be buried in Ramallah because Israel had barred him from being buried in Jerusalem. Although Palestinians seemingly adored Arafat, he failed to establish a true state for them, and hostilities with Israel have continued. Many non-Palestinians hoped that his departure might open the way to fruitful negotiations.

Photograph by Stephanie Sinclair Corbis

Nov. 17 President Vladimir Putin says that Russia is **developing nuclear missiles** unlike those of other nations. He states that the new weapons will be "put in service within the next few years" and be "of the kind that other nuclear powers do not and will not have."

Nov. 17 Radiocarbon dating of charcoal flakes from a fire pit found near Barnwell, S.C., suggests they are roughly 50,000 years old. Some scientists are skeptical about the age of the find, but if true it would put humans in the Americas 35,000 years earlier than has been believed.

Nov. 19 Fred Hale Sr., **the world's oldest known man,** dies in his sleep in suburban Syracuse 12 days before his 114th birthday. A lifelong Boston Red Sox fan, he lived long enough to see them win the World Series—again.

Friend or Foe?

It has been said that door-to-door fighting against urban guerrillas is among war's most intense endeavors, with every portal a potential peril. The combat that began on November 7 in Fallujah, a city of 350,000, was no exception. This battle, perhaps the most significant of the entire war, was launched to eradicate the insurgents' base of operations in Fallujah, with the goal of permitting Iraq to hold a real election in the future. More than 3,000 insurgents were killed or captured in the action, and some 71 Americans died. At least 650 homemade bombs, of the type hidden along roadways traveled by U.S. forces, were discovered. Here, on November 23, members of the Light Armored Reconnaissance, 1st Battalion, 3rd Marines, confront yet another situation.

Photograph by Scott Peterson Getty

Nov. 21 At the onset of the hunting season a dispute comes to a **bloody end** in Wisconsin. After a group of deer hunters tells an intruder that the deer stand he is using is on private property, and that he must leave, the man allegedly opens fire, killing six and wounding two. The suspect, Chai Vang, claims self-defense but is charged with six counts of murder and two counts of attempted murder.

Nov. 22 British TV news says that a **September 11–style attack** on Heathrow Airport and buildings in London's financial district has been thwarted. The British Home Office and Metropolitan Police have no comment on the report, which doesn't specify when the plot was to be executed.

Nov. 25 Heritage turkeys, which were driven from the market in the 1960s by mass-produced brands, grace many a Thanksgiving table today. More flavorful because they are raised on **a diverse diet,** these gobblers are making a comeback among gourmet cooks in the know.

Out of Control

Sports in America are a big deal. For many people, how their team does is a "life and death matter." There is a ton of money involved, and a lot of jobs. The players are heroes to kids, who routinely emulate them. So it was a disquieting event when on November 19 some of the Indiana Pacers, notably Ron Artest (right), fought with fans in the stands and on the court. Similar brawls have occurred before, in baseball, hockey and football as well, but this one, at least for now, is going to serve as the poster boy for disgraceful behavior. The players, as professionals, should have retained their composure. However, the behavior of some of the spectators was at least as frightening. It has been suggested that this is a sign of the times. If so, and the worst is yet to come, our society will be in for some unpleasant episodes.

Photograph from Getty

Dec. 1 Two hours before she is to be executed, Frances Newton receives a **four-month reprieve** from Texas Governor Rick Perry so that her lawyers can use new technology to conduct tests on evidence in the case. Newton was convicted 17 years ago of killing her husband and two kids.

Dec. 2 New York Yankees slugger Jason Giambi admitted in grand jury testimony that he had injected himself with human growth hormone and taken **steroids,** according to the *San Francisco Chronicle.* Giambi said he got the steroids from Greg Anderson, the personal trainer for superstar Barry Bonds of the San Francisco Giants. Bonds, who is in the process of rewriting baseball's record books, has denied any steroid use.

In a red-hot race for the White House, there would be plenty of spin, speculation and, of course, polls. But ultimately the democratic process speaks for itself.

Win, Lose or Draw
The gloves were off when the candidates met for three televised debates—in Coral Gables, Fla.; St. Louis; and Tempe, Ariz. (right, with moderator Bob Schieffer). Despite the mostly sound-bite answers, some voters said they felt better informed following the exchanges. The general response was that President Bush appeared a mite fidgety, while Senator Kerry seemed to retain his composure. There was no knockout blow delivered by either man, and the race remained close.

Charles Ommanney/Contact

And Then There Was One

By the end of the primaries it was clear: John Kerry had his party's nomination in hand. But at the beginning of the process, there was a slew of Democratic contenders, some familiar, some not, crowding the field. Connecticut Senator and former vice presidential candidate Joe Lieberman tossed his hat into the ring again, but with scant result. The Reverend Al Sharpton spoke his beliefs loud and clear, but not too many listened. Little-known former Vermont Governor Howard Dean made a big splash, then sank fast after he exploded in Iowa. Above, in Pittsburgh, Kerry, with wife Teresa, is en route to make the announcement that former primary rival John Edwards will be his running mate. At right, Kerry plays with Edwards' children Jack and Emma Claire.

On the Campaign Trail

The Kerrys welcome John and Elizabeth Edwards to Rosemont Farm, outside Pittsburgh, on the day that Edwards joined the ticket. Flying from Fort Lauderdale to New York, Kerry strums a guitar while senior adviser David Morehouse goes over a copy of the Democratic challenger's speech.

Four More Years

Opposite: Bush was running hard at an Albuquerque rally in August. Above, the President and wife Laura acknowledge supporters later that month at the Republican National Convention at Madison Square Garden in New York City. When the election finally came, on November 2, the networks were understandably eager to avoid the rash blunders of 2000. But by the next morning it was certain that George W. Bush had secured a second term, as victories in Ohio and Florida helped him land 286 electoral votes to Kerry's 252. At right, daughters Jenna and Barbara, along with Mom and Dad, are all smiles after the President delivers his victory speech in Washington, D.C.

Paul J. Richards/AFP/Getty

PORTRAIT | Tom Brokaw

One of television journalism's Old Guard signs off, and takes with him a sense of decency that has become all too rare. But we viewers must shackle our own selfishness and permit him to enjoy a new phase in his life.

Courtesy of the Brokaw family

Live, from the University of South Dakota radio station in 1962, at left. The future chronicler of the greatest generation, at age three, beneath protective headgear. With Meredith, his high school friend, college sweetheart and wife, heading to Woody Allen's New Year's Eve party in 1979. Opposite, his first of many days behind the NBC news desk, here as a host of the *Today* show.

Ron Galella

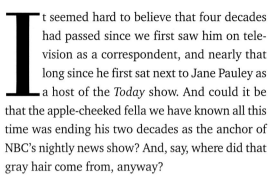

I t seemed hard to believe that four decades had passed since we first saw him on television as a correspondent, and nearly that long since he first sat next to Jane Pauley as a host of the *Today* show. And could it be that the apple-cheeked fella we have known all this time was ending his two decades as the anchor of NBC's nightly news show? And, say, where did that gray hair come from, anyway?

It seemed he would just always be there. After all, he has covered every American presidential campaign since 1968 and won countless honors (including a Peabody and seven Emmys). And though his dedication and reporter's instincts made him look lucky, he worked hard to be in the right place at the right time. He was front and center for the fall of the Berlin Wall and Nelson Mandela's release from prison. He conducted interviews with Mikhail Gorbachev and the Dalai Lama. Through it all, he never forgot his roots. And we liked that about him.

Born February 6, 1940, in Webster, S.D., Brokaw was the only kid a local store owner could trust to keep his hands out of the till during a summer job. "It just never would have occurred to me," he said. Of course it wouldn't. That innate trustworthiness is what viewers savored. He just seemed like a good guy, a regular guy, someone who wouldn't high-hat you. And despite the gray hair, we continually caught glimpses of that boy. Perhaps Brokaw's friend Nora Ephron summed it up best: "If Jimmy Stewart were an anchorman, he'd be Tom Brokaw."

He had a good run as the face of NBC, but it was a big job and with it came sacrifices. After a brief visit with his grandkids, he said, "I'm kind of a fly-by grandparent, and I don't like that very much." Leaving the anchor's chair will also mean seeing more of Meredith, his wife of 42 years, and the couple's three daughters. He will have more time for writing (another *The Greatest Generation*?) and such disparate passions as climbing.

The good news is that Brokaw isn't disappearing from our lives completely. He just wants to shift gears and become involved with longer forms. Thus he will appear in at least three NBC specials in 2005. So, he won't be there every night, but when we do see him, at least it will be for a longer time.

Christopher Little/Corbis/Outline

Although Brokaw declined President Clinton's 1993 offer to run the National Park Service, he is an avid outdoorsman (at left, with Abbie and Sage). Free from the breakneck pace of a daily show (below, at a production meeting in New York City, and, opposite, on the set), he relishes the prospect of time away from the office.

Charlie Archambault/U.S. News & World Report/Polaris

Christian Witkin

Carl Mydans

One of the primary shapers of photojournalism, he was the fifth photographer to join the LIFE staff, and forever demonstrated an uncanny ability to capture a story in a single shot. During his broad career, he produced memorable images of dust-bowl farmers and also of such celebrities as Ezra Pound and William Faulkner. His World War II photography is exceptional, with sharp images of the Japanese destruction in China and the Philippines. In fact, it was in Manila that he and his beloved wife, Shelley, a writer, were captured and imprisoned for nearly two years. After a POW exchange he went back to the war and took one of the 20th century's most celebrated pictures—MacArthur returning to the Philippines. Carl was 97. Here, in Italy in 1944, he is on the left and his friend for decades to come, George Silk, is on the right.

George Silk

Born in New Zealand in 1916, he was taking pictures with the Australian Army in WWII when he was captured by Rommel's troops, then escaped. He ended up working for LIFE during the war (and would ultimately be on staff for 29 years). Ashamed not to actually be fighting, he said, "I drove myself to show the folks at home, as best I could, how the soldiers lived and died." His efforts met with sterling results. After the war George became a noted sports photographer and later developed a "strip" camera that produced unusual, highly effective pictures.

David Douglas Duncan

Richard Avedon

Describing his starkly iconic portraits of the famous he said, "I have a white background. I have the person I'm interested in and the thing that happens between us." What happened, whether Richard Avedon was shooting President Dwight D. Eisenhower or Tina Turner, was uniquely revelatory. Though he captured such subjects as the Chicago Seven, civil rights workers and western drifters, Avedon's fashion work and portraiture proved to be his lasting trademarks. The first staff photographer at *The New Yorker,* he was on assignment for the magazine when he died at 81. Avedon considered his taking pictures almost every day for six decades to be his greatest achievement.

DOVIMA WITH ELEPHANTS PARIS 1?

Henri Cartier-Bresson

Known as the Eye of the 20th Century, he detested pretense (when traveling Stateside he used the alias Hank Carter). He always relied on available light and used his 35mm camera to snap singular pictures at "the decisive moment." This phrase refers to his notable knack for instantly capturing the essence of an event while simultaneously composing a shot of considerable impact. Born outside of Paris to wealth, Cartier-Bresson photographed world events, from the Chinese revolution to Mahatma Gandhi's funeral. But his frames also found magic in the everyday. Decades before his death at 95, he retired from photography and returned to his first love: drawing. Of his former career, Cartier-Bresson remarked, "It doesn't interest me."

WGBH-TV

SERIES

THE FRENCH CHEF

306   PROGRAM

To Roast A Chicken

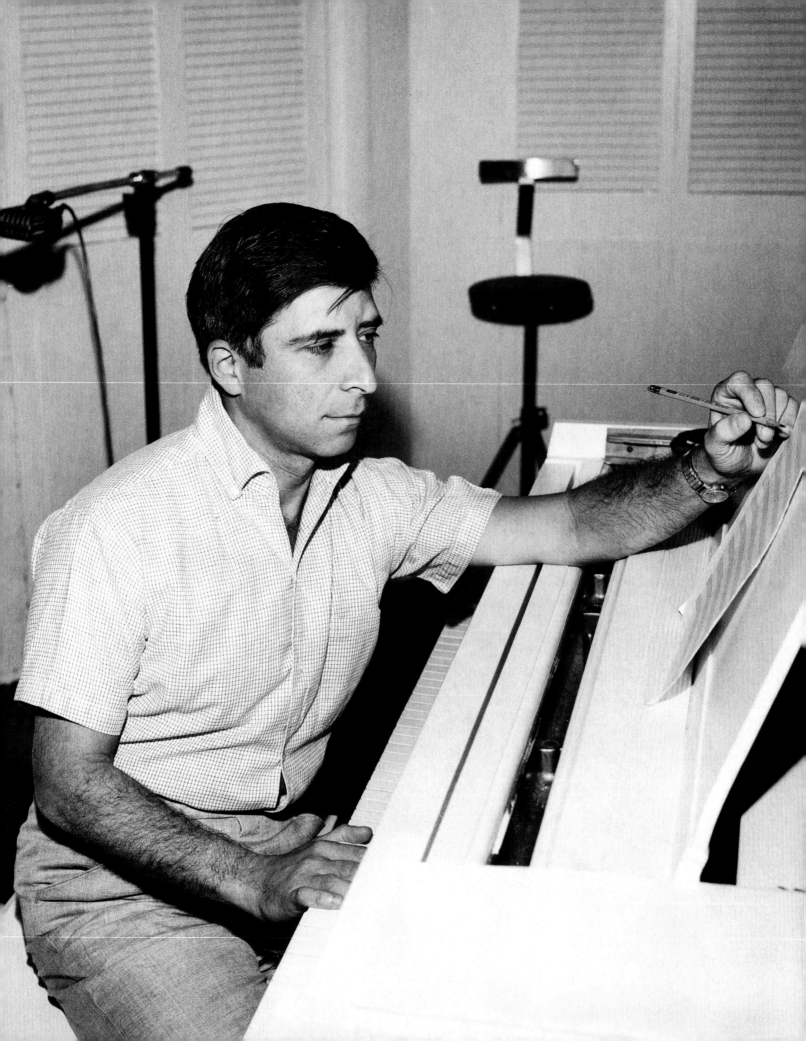

William Claxton/Courtesy of Demont Photo

Elmer Bernstein

He was a painter, a dancer and an actor before becoming one of the century's preeminent creators of motion-picture music. Over five decades, he provided the themes for more than 200 movies, sometimes outclassing the director in the process. In the 1950s, he dismissed the notion that film composition need be lush when he made *The Man with the Golden Arm* pulse with urgent, urban tones that perfectly captured the plight of a junkie. But he was also a master of the lyrical, as with the music for *To Kill a Mockingbird*. The themes from *The Magnificent Seven* and *The Ten Commandments* rank among the world's most familiar melodies. Bernstein, who died at 82, said he would run the rough cut of a film over and over until finally "it will start to talk to me. It will tell me stuff . . . Then you have something that fits, some sense of integration . . . instead of just slapping some wallpaper at the end."

David Raksin

Born in Philadelphia in 1912, he had his own radio dance band by age 12. In 1935 he ventured to Hollywood to work with Charlie Chaplin on *Modern Times,* and would go on to compose music for more than 400 movies and TV shows. However, it is a single melody—the one that Cole Porter said he would most like to have written—for which Raksin will be remembered. Others had turned down the chance to score *Laura,* the classic 1944 film noir directed by Otto Preminger and starring Gene Tierney and Dana Andrews. Raksin accepted the job, but when he went home he found a note from his wife saying she was leaving him. He then sat down and created the moody, dreamlike theme heard over and over in the movie, making it a masterpiece of mystery. Hedy Lamarr had been offered the title role but passed on it. As she later explained, "They sent me the script, not the score."

Gordon Cooper

A member of the Mercury Seven, the original American astronauts who carried the banner for the U.S. in the cold war space race and were immortalized in Tom Wolfe's *The Right Stuff*, Cooper was a classic, seat-of-the-pants pilot who set several endurance records in space (he was the first astronaut to sleep there) and was the last person to orbit the earth alone. Asked who was the best fighter pilot he ever saw, Cooper replied, "You're looking at him." He later claimed that NASA politics kept him from walking on the moon. An outspoken believer in UFOs, he was 77.

Robert Merrill

Born Moishe Miller in Brooklyn, Robert Merrill began his career at the Metropolitan Opera in 1945, and during his 31-year tenure there, he would perform virtually every baritone role. Not one to be typecast, the former semipro baseball pitcher built a career offstage as well. He was, perhaps, most well known for singing the national anthem at Yankee Stadium on Opening Day, a gig the affable Merrill kept for three decades. Said Yankees' owner George Steinbrenner, "His voice became synonymous with the stadium and with our team." Merrill was 87.

Jack Paar

He invented one of television's sturdiest genres: the late-night talk show. In 1957, NBC handed *The Tonight Show* to Paar, and he made it a must-see for five years. Before Paar, Steve Allen had been the host, but back then it was a variety show. Paar did have entertainers on, but the program mainly consisted of him talking to guests from all facets of society. He was an engaging fellow, very witty, nimble, warm and interested in all sorts of things. And his utter unpredictability gave the show a wicked edge. Tears were not unusual; he said he could cry "taking the Coca-Cola bottles back to the A&P." After the network edited out one of his jokes, he quit on camera. When he returned a few weeks later, he began, "As I was saying, before I was interrupted . . ." Paar, who indulged his love of travel for the past 30 years, was 85.

Alan King

The quintessential Jewish comedian called the Long Island Expressway "the world's largest parking lot" long before this metaphor became cliché. He was born in 1927 and quit high school to pursue stand-up. Often described as "an aggressive Jack Benny," he delivered his monologues with a cigar, jutted chin and Noo Yawk–tough gruffness. He appeared often on *The Ed Sullivan Show* and frequently subbed for Johnny Carson on *The Tonight Show*. King also appeared as a character actor in 29 films, of which he groused that he "was always the sergeant from Brooklyn named Kowalski."

JUST ONE MORE

Since time immemorial, the sight of locusts has hardly been a happy one, and in 2004 the insects did their inevitable damage in several countries. But also as ever, the sight and sound of children playing, of innocents living for the moment, is one of life's great joys. Here, in the Senegalese capital of Dakar, these kids are immersed in a sea of delights.